An Evacuee In The Hay
and other stories

by

E. J. Stapleton

An Evacuee In The Hay and other stories

Copyright © 2012 E.J.Stapleton

ISBN: 1478382716

ISBN-13: 978-1478382713

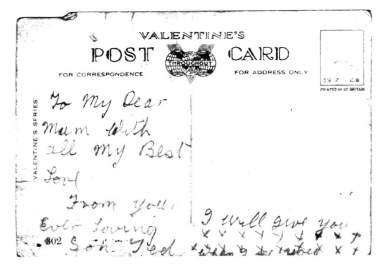

Postcard sent home in 1940 (rear)

For
Kate Kedwards
1882-1970

(Suffer little children)

Postcard sent home in 1940 (front)

Acknowledgements

There would not be enough space on this page to individually thank the many people that have helped me with this project. However, I would like to acknowledge the contributions of my daughter Sally Scott, my daughter in law Julie Stapleton, and my friend Sally Llewellyn for all their efforts in re-writing many passages and setting out pages and headings while trying to instil in me some knowledge on the intricacies of computers.

A very special thank you must go to my very good friends Roger and Ria Phillips, who took on the task of collating all the bits and pieces, and in spite of my sometime unreasonable demands for alterations have brought this project to fruition.

Further to the above, I must thank my friend and mentor, Sasha Clarkson, for all his work in reformatting the text and pictures to Amazon's Kindle and CreateSpace standards.

Incidentally, Roger Phillips' mother Stella (maiden name Williams) was born in Hay. Her parents ran the Wheatsheaf Public House and her grandparents had the Old Black Lion, both in Hay .

Small world!

E.J. Stapleton

Tenby 2012

Contents

Foreword   3

The Beginning   5

Bondy's   11

Life with Auntie Kit   17

Hay Double Three   26

In Love   28

The Pony   29

The Trolley   34

Pocket Money   40

Christmas 1943   43

The Return   47

Hay Changes   50

The Author   52

Disclaimer

This book is a recollection of my early boyhood, and some of the memories may have been distorted by time.

Foreword

In Hay cemetery, just behind the little gatehouse, in plot M1, lies the grave of one time Hay grocer Caleb Kedwards, and his wife Mary Ann. Also in this plot, without any outward sign or acknowledgement, are buried the remains of Calebs' Niece Kate Kedwards, Spinster of this parish.

You may question the relevance this has to these tales of wartime Hay. I would answer, that Kate Kedwards was the lady I knew as Auntie Kit, and although already a full time carer of her aged Mother, and not a young woman herself, took me in, an unhappy seven year old orphan, and gave me three and a half years of unstinting love and affection.

Kate Kedwards was born in Evesham, Worcestershire in 1882, and was brought up along with her younger Sister Dora, at 95 the High Street, St. Lawrence. Her Father, William Henry Kedwards was, at that time a solicitor's clerk, so Kate and her Sister probably had the genteel upbringing and education of the higher classes in the Victorian Era. Certainly, they would have been taught music, painting, needlework, and the etiquette required of young ladies of that time.

Sometime in the late eighteen hundreds, Kate moved to Hay to live with her Uncle Caleb and his wife Mary Ann. Caleb Kedwards, the younger Brother of Kate's Father, was then in business as a grocer. How, and when he came to Hay is not known. In 1885 at the age of Thirty Seven, he married Mary Ann Williams age Thirty, and employed her Nephew, Thomas Williams as his assistant.

We can only surmise the reason for Kate's move to Hay. Perhaps it was to assist Caleb's wife in running the house, or maybe she just wanted to get away from a cloistered life in Victorian Evesham. Whatever the reason; the 1901 census finds Kate, age nineteen, Caleb, and Mary Ann; together with Thomas Williams, living at 22 Broad Street Hay, which was probably the grocers shop. In 1911 Caleb's wife died, and soon after that Caleb retired and bought, or leased the house known as Ingle Nook, Church Street. Kate continued to keep house for him, and after her Father died in 1915, her Mother, Fanny Matilda, moved to Hay to be looked after by her daughter.

Some would say that Kate was committed to a life of drudgery, because in those days there was no such thing as refrigerators, washing machines, or central heating, so life must have been quite a struggle. Her Uncle Caleb died in 1936 aged 88, leaving Kate to carry on caring for her aged Mother. There, we leave Kate until the war years, when I, an evacuee from the London blitz came into her life.

Grave of Caleb Kedwards, Hay Cemetery

The Beginning

Three weeks we had waited, three weeks of that hot August of 1939. That we were going was certain, but when or where to, nobody knew. Not even my Mum, or Win and Doll, my two big sisters, and I thought that they knew everything.

Every day for the last week of August, we had struggled to school at Snowfields in Bermondsey with our belongings packed in brown paper carrier bags, ready to go at a moments notice. Then; after hanging about in the hall for a couple of hours we would be told "not today children", and the older kids went to their class rooms, while us little ones played about in the hall and made a lot of noise.

In the afternoon we were sent to sit next to our older Brothers and Sisters, where we would nod off to the drone of the teachers voice. I could never understand why we couldn't lay on the little yellow beds, like we used to before the threat of war came. At Four o'clock we would traipse back home.

Home was a two up and two down small terraced house in Richardson Street, off Long Lane Bermondsey, not far from the Borough underground station. A scullery in the rear led to a small yard and the outside lav, and that was it.

My Father died in 1933, when I was three months old, and my Mother, at age twenty eight was left to bring up three small children on just a small widows pension. So as soon as we were old enough she went to work at the Post Office headquarters in Mount Pleasant. She had to work early morning and late night shifts, so that she could always be there for us when we came home from school.

At last the great day came. On the first of September 1939 we walked in a long crocodile to London Bridge station. There; with hundreds of other children from several different schools we were put on trains along with our teachers, and started a journey that would change our lives forever.

After what seemed like an age we arrived at our destination, and were taken to a community hall, where we sat on the floor around the walls, and were given packets of biscuits and cups of tea. Although we didn't know at the time we were now in the seaside town of Seaford in Sussex.

Later; we were put into cars a few at a time and driven around the town calling at different houses so that people could select who they wanted to take in. In spite of the strict instructions that my Mother had given to my Sisters (i.e."Don't let him out of your sight.") I immediately lost sight of them, and found myself along with a boy of my own age name of Henry Tilley, the last two in the car.

After two or three rejections we called at a large detached house in Salisbury Road. A very smart woman came down the path to look us over, and after complaining that she "really would have preferred girls,"decided that she would take a chance and took the two of us in. It turned out that we were very lucky.

Winnie Glenister was the wife of a local bank manager. She only ever called him Glen, so we never new his real name. Both in their mid-forties and without children of their own they were by our standards very wealthy. The large detached house stood on a corner plot with lawns and flower beds at the front, and a kitchen garden at the rear. At the side of the house a short drive led to the integral garage that housed a smart blue 10hp Standard motor car with a Union Jack on the bonnet. To top it all they had a maid, Mary, who came in every day to do the chores and wait at table.

I'm convinced that Mrs Glenister really thought that this windfall of two little boys were hers' to keep. That afternoon she fussed over us like a mother hen, plying us with bananas and oranges, fruitcake, biscuits, sweets, and other goodies the like of which we had never seen. Later, with the aid of Mary, we wallowed in the real bath, while Winnie tut-tutted and nearly came to tears when she realised that our meagre belongings didn't run to pyjamas or nightshirts. Over the next couple of weeks the two little boys became the almost identical twins, Edward and Henry, which took a bit of getting used to on my part as my Mother always called me Teddy.

At a large department store in Eastbourne we were fitted out with every article of clothing and footwear that we would ever need for Winter or Summer, after that we were driven everywhere to be shown off to all and sundry as her boys. She tended to drive everywhere at top speed, often berating other road users with, "what's this fool doing in front now?" or, "go on if you're going and get out of the way!" Mr Glenister didn't drive and if he should happen to criticise her driving in anyway, even if it was just a gentle, "do be careful Winnie," she would tell him off in no uncertain terms. "Look here Glen! I don't need you to tell me how to drive my own car." Then she would give us boys a wink in the rear view mirror.

Mr. Glenister was a real gentleman, he had what you would call a "military" bearing, very upright and smart with a neat moustache. At weekend he would wear plus fours and a tweed cap and go off to play golf. He tended to call us "Old boys" or "Young shavers" and although he was in charge of a bank I think he was a bit under the thumb at home.

To my great joy I had found that my sisters were billeted three houses away with a Mr and Mrs May, so I was able to be in contact with them most of the time, also my mother came to see us every few weeks and take us off for the day. I missed my Mother very much and longed for her visits, because although the Glenisters' gave me every material need I can never remember having a cuddle or a kiss. When it was time for my Mother to go home, Mrs Glenister would drive us all to the station, then she would race the train to a level crossing near Newhaven so that we could give Mum a last wave. Quite a sport was Winnie!

Our stay in Seaford was not to be very long. In the late Summer of 1940 the battle of Britain was at its height, and the Germans were dropping bombs all along the south coast. It was all very exciting for us kids watching the dog fights as our fighters battled it out with Jerry. I can't remember ever being scared, the only trauma I suffered was when I had my tonsils taken out at a hospital in Brighton, but the powers above thought it all too dangerous, so we were all sent off to different destinations.

I say all, but for some reason I was left behind, maybe the Glenister's were pleading with the authorities for my adoption, in the event it was three weeks later that I was sent to join my Sisters in the market town of Hay on the borders of Herefordshire, and Breconshire, (now Hay on Wye) and so started another chapter of my life. By that time I was nearly seven years old.

Edward (left) and Henry: 'Twins' at Eastbourne

In the Garden

Seven Sisters Bay, Sussex

Ten Horsepower Standard

Bondy's

First day at Bondy's with my Sisters

I can't remember the actual journey from Seaford to Hay, only that I arrived by train in the evening and was met by a lady who walked with me up through the town to Market Street, where to my relief I was reunited with my sisters at the home of the widow Bondy, who was at that time in business as a furrier and wool merchant.

Mrs Bondy's small house was sandwiched between two warehouses that were her business premises, the larger one on the castle square end is now a collection of antique shops, and the other later became the forces canteen, and is now the British Legion. It was a gloomy cramped old place; the only room that received any daylight was the kitchen at the rear which had a glass roof., and as Mrs Bondy wasn't too house-proud the place was always in a mess, not helped by the two untrained cats that had the run of the place and did their business wherever they wanted.

After the pristine luxury of Seaford this all came as a bit of a shock, especially to my sisters who had also become terrified of the guard dog "Dino" a large brindled Great Dane with a ferocious bark that roamed the warehouses at night. So after a few tears and tantrums it was decided that my sisters were to be moved out, Dolly going to Dr. Powell in the the Bull Ring, (now Kilverts) and Winnie taken in by Mr Nut the chemist who owned the nice house that stands at the junction of Church St and Forest Rd. So I was left alone again and not very happy.

Despite all outward appearances Mrs. Bondy was not a poor woman, the large black Armstrong-Siddeley saloon car housed at the back of the larger warehouse was proof of that. It was looked after by her chauffeur/handyman, a big ginger fellow by the name of Faney Crompton, (Faney being short for Silvanum.) and at least once a week she would dress up to the nines and be driven off to Hereford or Brecon, sitting in the middle of the back seat like someone posh. I soon fell out with Faney after he gave me a clip round the ear for putting a wet brush on the newly polished wing of the car, (I was only trying to help) and learned to keep clear of him.

The only other employee was a man called Dick Price, everyone called him Gamme and he walked with a pronounced limp. I never did ask how he had got it, and he never spoke of it. He was short and tubby with grey hair and grey stubble on his chin, he had a habit of nibbling the inside of his mouth that made it look as though he was silently talking to himself. He spent a lot of his time writing in a large ledger whilst sitting birdlike on a tall stool at an equally tall desk that stood on a little platform under a window. He mostly worked in his shirt sleeves and waistcoat, but when there was other work to do he would roll up his sleeves and tie a sack under his armpits to use as an apron.

He talked a lot of his younger days, swimming and fishing in the Wye, and how dangerous it was to swim in the Steeple Pool, which was supposedly as deep as the church steeple was high. "When the river is running high" he said, "there's a cold current that can take you right down to the bottom and hold you there until your drowned." He also told me the tale of the bell from the church that was lost in the steeple pool years ago while being transported down river to be recast, and how if you heard the bell ringing in your ears when swimming you were drowning. I remember asking him if he had ever heard the bell ringing. "Course not," he had laughed and ruffled my hair. "Course not, I wouldn't be here to tell you the tale if I had, now would I?"

Apart from the occasional fox pelt the largest part of Mrs Bondy's business was dealing in rabbit skins. They arrived in their hundreds from butchers in the town, and from farmers and gamekeepers from the surrounding countryside. She also did a good trade with local poachers who always called after dark with a few skins, probably obtained on the previous nights outing. These, and other individuals would be paid spot cash, no questions asked. All the skins were thrown into a wheeled bin outside the back door, and when there was enough to make it worth while it was trundled into the warehouse and placed at the end of a large bench, where Gamme would begin operations. The skins were laid out on the bench twenty at a time where each had a handful of salt rubbed into it, then after three or four hours the salt would be scraped out taking most of the moisture from the pelt with it. Later they would be stretched onto wooden frames and hoisted up into the roof space to continue the curing process which took about three weeks.

After a few days dozens of large maggots began to fall from the skins, bouncing on the oily floor and crawling in all directions. It became my job to collect them up in a jam jar, then transfer them to a sweet jar half-full of sawdust that was kept on a shelf behind the desk. Gamme would later sell them to fishermen, I suppose it was one of his perks of the job.

All this was a continuous process and a record of each batch was kept in the ledger, so that it was known at what date they should be brought down and baled up ready to be sold on. A horrible smell pervaded the whole place, something that stayed with me for a very long time.

A few months into my stay at Bondys I realised that I had not heard Dino the dog barking and howling at night as was usual, so one morning just after breakfast and still clutching a crust of bread and jam I opened the door to the small warehouse and slipped inside.

All the windows were covered with sacking, and it took a few moments for my eyes to adjust to the gloom then all I could see were piles of poo dotted all over the floor. Suddenly a scuffling noise to my right made me turn to see the great dog rising from his bed of old blankets and coming towards me. He didn't bark or growl, the only sound was the scraping of his paws on the boards as he came up to me. Startled, I stepped back against the door which promptly clicked shut, trapping me. I was petrified and could hardly breathe; I had never been so close to him and never realised how big he was.

His head was as high as my chest, and the great jaws began to slobber and drool. I soon realised that he was staring at the crust that I still held so tightly that the jam had begun to squeeze between my fingers. I held it out to him but at the last moment lost my nerve and dropped it on the floor, he stooped and bolted it down in a instant then looked at me for more, I showed him my empty hand and his big tongue lolled out and licked off the rest of the jam, then to my great relief his tail gave a couple of slow wags. I left after promising to come to see him again.

After that I made a habit of popping in to see him every day or so, always taking some scrap or other for him to eat. He became quite friendly and would allow me to put my arm around his neck while I talked to him, sometimes I would hold on to his collar and lead him up and down the warehouse in and out of his piles of poo, but after a couple of rounds he would begin to pant and wheeze and wanted to lie down.

He was old and ill, all skin and bones, and although I knew this, I was still shocked one morning to find him gone, and the place all clean and tidy. I rushed to find Gamme and asked what had happened. "Ah, he was a sick old dog him son," he said, " and the Missus said that she couldn't afford to keep him any longer as how he wasn't any good at guarding nothing see, so she's had him put down." At this I burst into tears, and although he tried placate me by saying. " He didn't feel much, they just go to sleep see," I was too upset to listen.

Whether or not my late arrival in Hay was the reason, or I had just been forgotten, I had not been to school since I had been there, and as Mrs. Bondy didn't seem too worried about my welfare I found myself left much to my own devices.

The loss of my friend Dino hit me hard and I began to sink into my own little hell, becoming an unkempt scruffy little urchin. I took to wandering about the warehouse late at night, and became almost as wild as the family of feral cats that were allowed to live up among the beams and ledges to keep down the vermin, try as I might I never succeeded at making friends with any of them. I often cried myself to sleep hoping and praying that my mother would come and take me home, what's more I began to wet the bed, which didn't go down too well with the lady of the house.

Although I didn't realise it, my salvation was at hand, Mrs. Bondy had decided to spend Christmas away, and I was to be farmed out for the holiday. So a week before Christmas 1941 I was taken down to number eight Church St., there to be greeted by a homely looking lady with grey hair and pink cheeks who took my hand as she spoke. "Hello Teddy, would you like a nice piece of cake?" I had arrived at Ingle Nook.

Life with Auntie Kit

That first day at Ingle Nook convinced me that this was the place for me, and I told myself that I would never go back to the rabbit skin warehouse what ever happened.

I must have been in a really scruffy state at the time because after I had scoffed the cake my new Auntie suggested that I might like to have a bath, to which I readily agreed, thinking that it would be a stand up in a tin tub job, but to my surprise she led me down a steep flight of wooden steps into the cellar where the bathroom was situated.

To call it a bathroom is a bit misleading because really it was just a six foot wide space partitioned off from the pile of coal that filled the rest of the cellar. There were duck boards by the side of the bath and a wooden stool at the end, a flimsy door with a couple of hooks on which to hang your clothes and afford a bit of privacy, and that was it, except for an ancient gas water heater that hung over the bath at the tap end that gave out a loud "Woof !" when lit, then coughed and spat out the hot water in dribs and drabs for a minute or two before warming up enough to give a smooth flow.

After that novel bath it was upstairs to have my hair dried and trimmed in front of the fire, in the end she gave me a girls fringe but I didn't care, I was already in love with her and willing to do whatever she asked.

Later she introduced me to her mother, a very old lady who spent all her days in an armchair in the front room; she was dressed all in black except for a pink shawl around her shoulders and a nightcap from under which a few wisps of silver hair had escaped. In all the time I was at Ingle Nook I can never remember holding a conversation with her; I suppose the difference in age and background made it impossible for us to have anything in common. [She died in 1951 aged 99.]

Inglenook, Church Street

All too soon my first day at Ingle Nook came to an end and it was bedtime, it was then that we had a small problem, on the half landing under the window was a plant stand on which rested an alabaster bust of Kate's uncle Caleb, the Roman type head had blind staring eyes that frightened me and I refused to go past, Auntie quickly resolved the problem by whipping the cloth from under it and draping it over its face.

Then after putting a towel on me like a nappy (just in case) she tucked me into bed, knelt and prayed, then sat and talked to me until I was ready to be left to sleep.

That first Christmas with Auntie Kit went by in a whirl, and I have only a hazy memory of it, one thing I do recall though is the Christmas tree which was about a foot high growing in its own pot with just a bit of tinsel wrapped around it. Later, I planted it in my own little garden plot where it grew to four or five feet by the end of the war.

After Christmas I started to worry about being sent back to the rabbit skin warehouse,and I pleaded with Auntie to let me stay with her only to be told that the social people didn't think she could manage to look after me and her mother any longer.

The fatal day came when the handover was to take place and on the pavement outside the house the social lady told me to thank Miss Kedwards for having me and then she would take me back to Bondy's, that was when I began to play up. She took my arm and started to lead me away but I broke free and ran crying back to Auntie pleading with her not to let them take me. The woman tried to drag me off, shouting that I was a naughty boy and shouldn't be behaving like this, but I would have none of it throwing myself on the ground in a tantrum, kicking and screaming at anyone that tried to get near me.

In the end a neighbour rushed out and helped the woman get me to my feet, still sobbing I threw my arms around Auntie's neck knocking her rimless glasses up onto her head, then through her own tears I heard her tell them, " I can't let him go like this, I'll have to keep him." Next minute we were up the steps and back in the house sitting side by side on the stairs where she held me close until I stopped crying, then she said, " It will be alright Teddy, I'll be your Auntie Kit and you'll be my Christmas baby." I was safe home and from there on my life would take a turn for the better.

Although around sixty years of age and a spinster Kate was well in tune to the needs of young people, she was the resident organist for the chapel at the bottom of Belmont, (now the Catholic Church) and had a lot to do with the town as an organiser of childrens outings, parties, and fancy dress parades. Apart from that she also taught piano, so there were always children about. Much to my regret in later life she could never get me to sit long enough to learn to play.

I believe that I was the child that Kate had longed for but could never have, she certainly treated me as if I were her own, and I soon became as big a part of her life as her mother. She had a way of making everything we did seem exciting, always ready to play cards or board games in the evenings, and joined me every afternoon in listening to childrens hour on the wireless, with Uncle Mac, Larry the lamb,and all their friends.

I quickly became her willing helper in the house, fetching coal from the cellar,and learning to lay the two fires that were the only form of heating in the house, apart from the small gas stove.

Like most country women at that time Kate baked her own bread and cakes, and I became adept at rolling pastry and cutting out welsh cakes, my reward was being allowed to scrape out the last of the cake mix from the bowl. All the other country ways came into being as the seasons went by, raspberries from the garden,and blackberries from the hedgerows became pots of jam, and the hazel trees at back of the warren provided enough nuts to fill a large sweet jar where they ripened and went brown in time for Christmas, while in my own aforementioned plot she got me growing lettuce, spring onions, radish for salads and shallots for pickled onions.

The School Room

I went back to school and quickly caught up with my neglected studies, and with her encouragement began to write home on a regular basis. I also stopped wetting the bed which was a bonus. School was the church hall in Heol-y-Dwr which had been adapted to take the influx of evacuees, the hall had been divided into different classes by green curtains hung on wires, so you were liable to be distracted from your own lessons by all the chatter going on around you. The highlight of the day for me was at break time in the morning, when teacher would dole out a large dollop of cod liver oil and malt from a cardboard drum of the stuff, we had to supply our own spoons which were soon licked clean.

It was at that school that I experienced the nastier side of some grown-ups.

In the phtograph of the hall there can be seen a small recess formed by a wall on the pavement side and the end of the building, (it's behind the lamp post.) In those days it was partitioned off to form the boys toilets, inside the door and to the left was a single cubicle w/c, and at the end the wall had been coated with tar to form a urinal. It was into there that I dashed one morning having been excused from class to use the toilet, and told to hurry up.

I soon found myself standing next to a giant coalman, I thought nothing of it and began to pee by lifting the leg of my shorts,the method used by all small boys whose shorts were not equipped with a fly. I felt a slight movement beside me that made me glance to my right,only to see the largest penis I had ever seen being waved gently to and fro before my eyes, such was its hypnotic effect that I could not take my eyes off it till a voice from above broke the spell.

" Do yer want to hold un son?"

I declined the offer with a shake of my head, so surprised and frightened that I couldn't speak, but just stared at the wall and dribbled down my own leg. Then came a nudge on my shoulder that made me look up at his face made ugly by coal dust that emphasised the pink rimmed eyes and reddend lips. "Go on hold un," he said, this sounded more like an order than a request to me, things were getting serious, should I comply, or refuse and risk something worse happening? In the event the decision was made for me. Suddenly the door crashed open and another kid came running in to take his place on the other side of my tormenter, almost before he had reached the wall I was racing away my feet hardly touching the ground as I flew out. I never told anyone of it, and I never found out what happened to the other kid. (Hopefully nothing.)

Throughout the rest of my boyhood I was always wary of using public toilets if men were hanging about outside, and always refused the invitations of the seemingly nice fellows that wanted to pay for you to go to the cinema.

Apart from this frightening incident my life at Ingle Nook became one long round of pleasure the whole town became my playground, at weekend or when not at school I would be found around the mart or down at the Swan well, I could wander all over the warren, go bird nesting along the baily walk or use Aunties old bike to scoot up and down the Forest Road. Down on Black Lion Green I could wade in the Dulas and try to catch the little fish that we called fat heads.

In bad weather I was content to spend hours reading in the old summer house at the top of the garden, it was empty save for an old bedstead, and the plasterboard lining was buckled and crumbling, but you could still make out the now faded beach scenes that she had painted long ago.

One of my favourite haunts was the Norman tump that is just down the street from Ingle Nook, there I often climbed to the top and pretended to be king of the castle, that is until the Home Guard installed an anti-aircraft gun inside a ring of sandbags on top, then I could only watch from afar as now and again an Airspeed Oxford aeroplane would make an attack on the town and the the gun atop the tump could be heard click click clicking furiously as the old boys pretended to shoot it down.

The war did not intrude in the life of Hay to any great degree except for the time when units of the American and British army became billeted in the town, which was great for us kids as we were able to cadge chewing gum and chocolate from the yanks, (got any gum chum?) and had the occasional ride in the bren-gun carriers of the British.

There was one other flurry of excitement when a stray bomb fell near a small farm called Cock-a-Lofty up on the bluff a couple of miles away, and a small crowd walked out the next day to look at the four-foot hole and a row of small dead birds that had been blown out of the eaves of the stone barn, and that was it.

Another great interest came into my life when Auntie persuaded me to join the cubs, and I became a member of the Ist Cusop Wolf-Cub pack and was soon fitted out with a smart green jersey, black shorts, and a nice blue and yellow scarf, which was held together by a leather woggle. The cub mistress (Akela) was Miss Mary Moore, who ran both cubs and scouts from her house in Cusop. The house is situated a little way up the Dingle on the right and is fronted by a small wall with short railings atop behind which was a small open courtyard, where we used to parade and be inspected on cub nights. (I say was, because the courtyard is now overgrown with bushes and shrubs.)

To the right of the drive there is a small coachhouse where we spent many happy hours making plasticine models and playing all the games that cubs would get up to, including all the little tasks and tests, such as tying knots, or lighting a camp fire; these could earn you different badges that were sewn on to the sleeve of your jersey. Miss Moore had the misfortune to be handicapped in that she had one leg shorter than the other and had to wear a built-up boot on the short leg, so she always wore a long hobble skirt to hide it from view, in spite of that she was as lively as a cricket and easily kept up with us youngsters most of the time.

At the end of the war the house became the property of Mr. Lance Hughes, a veterinary surgeon whose wife was a great friend of Mary Moore, and the coach house became part of the practice. While researching this work I had the good fortune to meet Mr.Michael Tunley of Cusop, who introduced me to Mrs. Lance Hughes who insisted that I had tea with her, while she told me about Mary Moore's Army family background showing me lots of old group photographs of the Generals in her family with their units, also in her possession were the helmet and ceremonial sword that belonged to one of them. It is believed that one of Mary's ancestors was General Sir John Moore of Corunna fame!

The memorial stone of my cub mistress

Hay Double Three

"**D**o you think I'll be able to do it?" The boy asked. "Of course you will!" Auntie replied. "It'll be easy, you'll see , now what time did she say."

"Five o'clock, I think that's what she said."

"Well it's nearly that now you had better go, here's the money." She pressed two large copper pennies into his hand. "Mind you don't lose it."

It was a late October evening, wet and misty, he shivered a bit as he left the warmth of the house and hurried to the top of church street where stood the red telephone box. He entered,and as the heavy door closed behind him he felt cut off from the outside world. The bright light inside was reflected in all the little windows that prevented him from seeing anything outside, all the glass was wet with condensation, and there was a puddle on the floor. The black box in front of him had a large white letter A at the top with a silver button beside it, at the bottom was a letter B with its button that you had to press to retrieve your money from a cup at the side if a call was not successful, on the top were slots where the money was placed when making a call, the only other thing in the box was a large telephone directory with a torn cover that sat on a shelf below the black box.

He lifted the heavy black reicever and pressed it to his ear, all he could hear was the sound of his own breathing, and his steamy breath formed little drops of water in the mouthpiece. Suddenly a ladies gentle voice spoke. "Number please.?" Startled! He looked around as though the voice was in the box with him, his mouth and throat went dry and he could only mutter " err err" The voice came again.

"What number do you require caller?" At last he found his voice. "Hay double three," he blurted. "Per, please." This time the voice gave an instruction. "Place two pence in the box caller." He realized that the money was still clutched tightly in his hand, and quickly pressed the coins into the slot. A long pause, then, "Press button A caller you're through." He pressed the button and heard the coins rattle down, then breathed a sigh of relief as a more familiar voice spoke. "Hello who's calling?" Two minutes later he was back in Ingle Nook.

"I've done it, I've done it!" he told her, his eyes shining in triumph. The woman he called Auntie smiled at him, her eyes twinkling through her rimless glasses. "Well done," she said, patting his head. "Well done, now what did she say?

"She said, hello who's calling, and I said its me Akela I said, and she said that I had done everything right and I've passed the test, and I'm to get the 'Using the Telephone' badge when I next go to cubs."

"That's very good," said Auntie. "You have done well, now wash your hands quick and sit up at the table, your tea's ready."

In Love

I fell in love when I was eight
With a girl I met at her garden gate
Along the Brecon Road.

Her Mother seemed to take to me,
And I was taken in for tea,
And questioned as to who I be,
And where was home.

We played together in fields nearby.
I taught her my new kite to fly,
Way up high into the sky.
Until the tow line broke.

The kite came down into a tree,
Much too high for little me,
And no way there that I could see
To get it down.

So; it wasn't those clear eyes of blue,
Or the glimpse of knickers, of similar hue,
or her rosy cheeks, or pigtailed hair,
That left me standing there to stare.

No; it was the way she shinned up that old oak,
Just like she was another bloke.
Brought my kite down safe and sound,
and smiling, laid it on the ground.
That's what made me fall.

The Pony

The boy was thin, almost skinny, but with a wiry toughness about him of a distance runner. Even with the approach of autumn he still wore summer clothes, just shorts, shirt, and open sandals. His limbs tanned through spending most of his time outdoors.

It was market day in The Hay, and he had followed his usual routine of wandering about the mart. Well used to the busy yards he was nimble enough to keep clear of cattle, carts, and lorries.

The animals were constantly being moved nearer to the auction ring. The sheep; when released from one pen would flow to the next like grey foam, heads pressed to their neighbours flanks, their hooves drumming on the little concrete slabs. The wild eyed slimy nosed cattle, not used to strangers, would back away at anyone's approach, heads lowered, snorting dragons breath into dark dank straw.

The market men, dressed in smocks or brown overall coats all carried sticks, and used them liberally. Even in the middle of conversation one would suddenly turn and give a passing beast a cut across its hind quarters, always accompanied by a, "Gid on there."

He thought it cruel, but not so cruel as the treatment given to the pigs. Every now and again a man in leather apron would climb into their pen, at which they would all start squealing at once. Then holding his selected victim between his knees, he would pin a tag to its ear with a pair of clippers that looked the same as the ticket collector used to clip tickets at the station.

He spent a long time looking at the ponies. Six of them this week, shaggy legged with mane and tails down to the ground, brought down from the mountain, still wild and wary. They were penned in on three sides in a corner of the yard, kept back from the entrance by one of the market workers.

He was a tall man with a grey stubbled chin and big red hands. His coat was kept closed by a length of hairy string tied around his waist. His boots were covered with flecks of yellow dung. With stick under arm and a greasy cap tilted back on his head, he leaned against the fence smoking a rolled up fag.

"What happens to these ponies?" the boy asked. "Where do they go?"

The man grinned, showing a row of tobacco stained teeth.

"Where do they go?" he echoed. "Why, for bloody cats meat boy, that's where."

The boy hurried away, the man's laugh ringing in his ears, sad at the ponies' fate.

Down Church Street he went, to the house where he lived with the woman he called Auntie. The bicycle that she let him use was leaning against the wall. It was a lady's model so although too small to reach the saddle, he was able to stand on the pedals as he rode along.

Down to the Forest Road he went, the lane that leads to Capel-Y-Ffin and Hay Bluff. There, with mart and ponies forgotten, he started on a more important and dangerous mission.

Set in the bank a few yards into the lane the wasps' nest that he had found a few days before had become the enemy camp, the bicycle was his bomber, his ammunition was a handful of gravel or a stone gathered from the side of the lane. His task was to ride quickly past, bomb the enemy camp, and be away before the wasps could retaliate.

He had just completed his third bombing run, and was waiting for the wasps to settle down, when into the lane trotted one of the ponies from the mart. Instinct must have told her that this was the way back to the mountain. She slowed a little on seeing him there, then came on, her unshod hooves making little noise on the rough surface.

The boy quickly laid the bike on the ground and stood with his arms held wide. She stopped, her head held forward sniffing the air. "Another few feet and I will be able to touch her" he thought.

For a few moments that seemed like an age they stood looking at one another until the spell was broken by a shout from the top of the lane. It was the man from the mart chasing after the escapee.

"Hold un, hold un," he shouted.

At the sound of that shout the pony bolted forward, trying to run between the boy and the bank. Without hesitation or thought of danger he threw himself at her, grasping her long mane as she passed. He was dragged a few yards, grazing his knees and toes, but his weight slowed her enough for the market man to catch up.

"Good boy" he panted, "good boy." Quickly he forced a rough noose over the pony's head and wrapped the loose end around his wrist.

"You've done good son, I'd never caught un without yer."

Then taking a few coppers from his pocket, he thrust them into the boy's hand, with, "Here, take this". The hero's eyes shone with pride. "Thanks mister, thanks".

He made to go, only to have his triumphant mood shattered by the pony's squeal of pain, and could only watch in horror as the man beat her again and again.

"I'll teach you to run" he shouted, as he landed another blow.

"Don't hit her, don't hit her" the boy cried. "You shouldn't do that."

"Wassamatter with you?" was the retort.

"I've give ya money, ain't I?"

The boy wanted to tell him to stop, to let her go, he didn't want the money. Fierce tears stung his eyes when he realised that he had stopped her from getting away, it was all his fault that she was being hurt, and would be made into cat's meat.

"Yer you" was all he could blurt out as he flung the coins at the man's feet.

"Yer daft bugger" the man laughed, and continued to drag his captive away.

Frustrated, the boy picked up a stone and was ready to throw it, when another plan entered his head. Picking up the bike he ran past the man and pony up to the wasp's nest, and waited until they were nearly level. Then, taking careful aim, he made a direct hit on the enemy camp. He ran as fast as he could, only stopping when he heard the bully's bellow. Looking back he saw that the man had dropped his stick and pony's head rope, and while he was trying to beat away a cloud of angry wasps, she was running off at a smart trot.

"Go, go" he heard himself shouting. "Go on, you'll soon be on the bluff".

The market man was shaking his fist, so the boy didn't wait, but rode down the bumpy path to the warren, and made himself scarce for the rest of the afternoon. Next morning, he went back to the Forest Road and found the money, but of course, he didn't raid the wasps' nest; they deserved to be left alone.

The Trolley

It had seemed ages that he'd been waiting. Every week, since the woman he called Auntie had arranged to have it made, the boy had called at the carpenter's workshop behind Garibaldi Terrace to see if it was ready. Every time he had called, the old man had greeted him in much the same way. "Not you again" he'd laugh. "Alright, you can come in, but it's not ready yet." Then; ruffling the boy's hair; "You're an impatient one you. Don't you know there's a war on?"

The boy would wait a few minutes, shuffling his feet through the shavings and sawdust, not liking to ask what the war had to do with it all. Then; disappointed, he would leave, saying,

"I'll come back next week then."

This week though it was all so different. The old man had nodded towards a corner of the workshop.

"Take a look under that there sheet."

The boy drew back the cover, and stood silent, taking in every detail. The box like seat, open at the front end, and the bottom boards; the middle of which extended forward to take the front axle, were all made of oak, and gleamed under a fresh coat of varnish. The wheels; ah the wheels, discarded pram wheels they were, with iron axles, solid white rubber tyres and shiny chrome hubs and spokes. The trolley could be steered by the feet of the driver, or by the stout rope reins that were attached to either end of the swivelling front axle. The bottom boards extended six inches from the back, so that anyone pushing could jump on and ride guard-like behind the driver. The brake, a solid oak shaft with a block on one end, was through bolted to the side, and when pushed forward rubbed against the back wheel. It was altogether the best trolley he had ever seen.

"Well, what d'yer think.?"

The carpenter's voice cut through his thoughts.

"Ere, it's good" was all he could say.

"Good! Is that all? Only good." The old man's voice filled with mock annoyance. "I thought it were better than that."

"Oh!, it is, it is," the boy was quick to reply." It's the very best, can I take it now?"

The carpenter grinned. "Alright, off you go, and if you fall off and break your leg, don't come running back to me." He laughed at his own joke, but the boy didn't hear. He was too busy pushing it up Oxford Road, and on reaching the down slope jumped aboard, and sped down past the Blue Boar into Church Street pulling up smartly outside the house called Ingle Nook. It was his at last, and it was going to be so much fun.

It was fun too; fetching his Auntie's shopping from Broad Street on market day, gathering loads of dried sticks from the hedgerows for fire lighting, and earning a few coppers into the bargain when running errands for neighbours'. When not engaged in any of this he would just enjoy riding about, and on finding that he could go from the top of Oxford Road, down Church Street, and almost as far as the Forest Road before stopping, would do it time and again trying to beat his own record.

All went well for a few weeks, until two older boys came to live at Ingle Nook. Peter and Ronnie were fourteen, and nearly ready to be sent back to London. Much to the boy's chagrin they took command of his beloved trolley, and most of his little jobs. Even his task of throwing crumbs from the bread board up onto the scullery roof for the birds was taken by Peter, who; with his first back-swing opened a cut on the boy's eyebrow, which required two stitches at the Doctor's surgery in Broad Street.

He complained of course; to the woman he called Auntie, but to no avail.

"You'll have to learn to share." She chided.

The boys' Auntie is ill, and can't keep them anymore. It's only for a little while, you'll see. Now you be good, and try to get on with them."

He did try, though without much success. Most of the time the older boys' just ignored him, but the day came when things changed, and he regained some control over events, even if it was in an unusual way.

It happened one Friday afternoon, when he had just finished listening to children's hour on the wireless, and was on his way up stairs when he heard a low murmuring from the boys' room. On peeping through the gap of the partly open door a strange sight met his eyes. Peter and Ronnie stood facing each other with their trousers around their knees. Peter had a small tin of vasaline in hand, the contents of which he was smearing onto his private parts with a slow gentle motion, while Ronnie; already coated up, was taking more vigorous action. Both nearly jumped out of their skins when the boy entered the room.

"What are you doing" he asked?

"Ere; we're just putting this on to make our hair grow," said Peter, hastily pulling up his pants.

"Yes, that's right" agreed Ronnie. "Makes your hair grow

see!" The boy wasn't convinced.

"Gar'n, your being dirty. I'm going down to tell Auntie."

"No, don't tell, don't tell." Ronnie's voice rose in panic."You don't want to get us into trouble do you?"

"Why don't you try some?" Peter offered. "You can get hairs too."

"Ugh! No; I don't want no hairs. It's naughty what your doing, and I'm telling."

He left the room with a passing shot.

"I bet you two will cop it when I tell her."

Of course he didn't tell, but waited until halfway through breakfast before making his play.

"I think it should be my turn for the trolley today, don't you Auntie" he asked casually?

"Yes" She agreed. "Why don't you boys give him a ride this morning?"

"Ere; yes," Peter was quick to answer; at the same time giving Ronnie a kick on the shin under the table. "We'll give him a good go today. Won't we Ronnie?"

"Oh! Oh yes," said Ronnie."We'll take him all around town, for as long as he likes."

The boy smiled to himself. He'd got them, good and proper.

True to their word, (although they didn't have much choice,) the boys gave him a good ride. Down as far as the cemetery and back, then up over Oxford Road, and down to the bridge at Cusop.

At the boy's insistence they pulled him up the Dingle, to say hello to Miss Moore, the cub mistress. Back again to town, and down onto Black Lion Green. There they stopped for a rest, while Ronnie; who had grown a blister; took off his dabs and cooled his feet in the Dulas Brook. Then off they went again, dragging the trolley with the boy sitting in, up the footpath that runs outside the town walls. The path was rocky, strewn with stones and gravel, and when they came to the top the boy began to have second thoughts about riding down the steep slope that lead to the bottom of Broad Street.

"I'll let you have a ride now Peter," he announced; jumping out of the seat.

"My bums gone a bit sore."

Peter gave him a knowing grin.

"I thought this one would be a bit too much for you. Don't worry, I'll drive; Ronnie can ride behind me, and you can push us off and jump on the back."

So the fateful ride began.

From the start it was going to be a disaster. Peter found that with Ronnie taking up so much of the seat, he was unable to get his feet up onto the front axle to steer, so asked him to "Shove back a bit." On hearing Ronnie's reply of "Ok," the boy; taking it as a signal to go, gave the trolley a good shove as instructed. Peters' cry of; "Wait, wait," was too late.

With the weight of the two boys aboard the trolley quickly gathered speed. Peter tried braking with his feet, only to have the crepe soles of his sandals ripped off by the rough surface. Ronnie applied the brake with such force that it broke the rubber tyre, which tumbled and writhed down the slope after them, like a white snake.

The boy, stumbling along behind, could only watch in horror as the trolley slammed into a rocky outcrop that protruded from under the walls, buckling the wheels, shedding the rest of its tyres, and finally coming to a shuddering halt against a gate post at the bottom.

Both boys were crying. Peter; because his legs had been forced under the front axle, skinning his shins from ankle to knee. While Ronnie had hurt his ribs, when falling against the brake handle with such force that it had broken away from the seat.

There was nothing else for it. They had to half carry, half drag the wreck along Broad Street and up Belmont, while enduring the jeers and taunts of some other kids, who were standing by the clock tower.

"You silly, silly boys!" Was all Auntie had said, as she bathed their wounds, thinking that the loss of the trolley and their pain was punishment enough.

"Put it up in the summer house, and we'll see what can be done."

Of course, nothing was done. In a few weeks Peter and Ronnie were gone, leaving the boy alone again. The trolley was never mended, and the only good thing that came out of it all was the brake handle. That became a marvellous make-believe tommy-gun for the rest of the war!

Pocket Money

Finding spending money was always a problem in the early years of my time in Hay, the few coppers earned running the odd errand didn't buy a great deal, and although Auntie Kit probably received an allowance for keeping an evacuee it couldn't have gone far, so she could only afford me the occasional sixpence or shilling.

I could always rely on a half a crown postal order from my Mother on birthdays but that didn't last more than a week or two. Sweets were only an occasional treat because not only were they hard to come by but also they were rationed so the few sweet coupons that we had didn't go far, so it was really only a couple of comics a week that my money would run to.

basement entrance to Grants on Belmont

Things became easier in later years after I managed to wangle myself a Saturday morning job at "Grants" Castle Street, the emporium that sold newspapers and magazines, books and stationary, china and glassware, haberdashery and general ironmongery. The tasks I was given varied from week to week: sometimes I would be helping to unpack crockery and glassware from straw filled crates that had been delivered to the shop via the basement, the doors of which opened out on to Belmont. Another week would see me helping out in the Grants large garden that ran from Belmont right down to the Bailey Walk.

I got on well with the old gardener until the day that I frightened the life out of him when I took a bite of his chewing tobacco that he had left on a bench seat. When he found me crying and foaming at the mouth he thought I was having a fit, and ran to the shop shouting for someone to fetch a doctor. In the end the doctor wasn't needed, but after that the old man wouldn't have me with him any more.

A more mundane task was to be sent up stairs to help Granny Grant clean the family cutlery, this involved having to wear an apron and rubbing the knives and forks with a damp cloth and brick dust. I don't suppose that there was much going in the way of stainless steel in those days.

The job that I enjoyed most was being set to dust and tidy up the stock in the stationary department, there I could read to my hearts content, but always ready to look busy if anyone came by. An added bonus of my job was that the kindly Mr. Grant allowed me to pick myself a present on my birthday, the first year I chose a kite, and the next, to his great surprise I selected a Victorian iron hoop, a batch of which I had found at the back of the cellar long forgotten by everybody. The waist-high hoop had an iron ring with a wooden handle that was permanently attached, so it never ran free and was always under control. I soon got the hang of it and could go everywhere at a fast trot.

Some unpaid work was quite enjoyable, we were sometimes taken up onto the bluff and into the surrounding fields by our teachers for nature rambles or picnics this usually turned out to be doing something for the war effort, like gathering sheep wool from hedgerows and barbed wire fences, or harvesting armfuls of "foxgloves," the dried leaves of which produce the drug Digitalis for medicinal use.

By far the best paid work was obtained on the local farms, where because of the manpower shortage children were always welcome to help out with hay-making and potato picking. Making hay was easy, after the grass had been cut it was drawn into long swaths with wooden rakes, then it was just a matter of walking up and down the field turning it over in the sun; first one way, then the other until it was bone dry and sweet smelling. At the end of the day it was tied up in bundles and carted off to fill the barn or to be built into hayricks.

Spud picking was heavier work but better paid, we were all issued with buckets and had to follow the great horse as he ploughed open the drill and left the potatoes on the surface, each bucketful had to be carried to the top of the field to be emptied into sacks, so by the time one drill was cleared the horse and plough would ready to open the next.

A big bonus on both jobs was the midday break when the farmers wife would come out with loads of sandwiches and billycans of tea. It was usually home made bread with the farmers own cured ham and was delicious. I can't recall what the rates of pay were at the time, but I do remember going home to London with five fifteen shilling certificates in my post office savings, that was about a weeks wages for some people in those days.

Christmas 1943

Christmas 1943 was to be my last at the Hay, and the most memorable. Not because it was any less frugal than those before, rationing and the shortage of almost every thing took care of that, but because I was now ten years old, growing up fast, and was able to take in a lot more of what was going on.

A fall of snow a week before Christmas gave me a good start to the holiday. I was fortunate in that my eldest Sister Winnie was billeted with Mr. Nutt the chemist who owned a large house on the Brecon Road, and I was allowed to play with his Son Bobby on the sloping field behind the house. Here we spent some happy hours riding on his real toboggan.

On coming back to Ingle Nook on that Saturday afternoon Auntie Kit bade me run barefoot in the snow. She told me that this was an old wives tale that would ensure that I would never suffer from chilblains. After a couple of turns around the garden my feet were freezing, but after she had given them a good towelling they became as warm as toast.

Next day, (Sunday) we went as usual to worship at the little Church at the bottom of Belmont. Auntie Kit was the organist there and I had become her assistant who worked the bellows of the wind driven organ. We were separated from the congregation by a green curtain, so I didn't have to take in much of the service, only to watch for my cue to get the pump handle going at the start of the next hymn.

Much of the week was taken up by the usual Christmas activities, a group of us from the church sang carols at the big houses on the Hereford road and up Cusop dingle, well wrapped up against the cold with scarves and home made balaclavas, crunching home in the dark on the frozen remains

43

of last weeks snow.

We made cheap paper chains with strips of coloured paper stuck together with paste made from flour and water. She made pastries and a small Christmas cake ready for the great day, how she managed to get all the ingredients together in those days of rationing I never knew.

That Christmas was the only time I can remember her ever being angry with me. A week or so before I had shown her a letter that I had written ready to send to my Mother, asking for a bike for Christmas. Auntie Kit promptly tore it up and threw it on the fire.

"You'll do no such thing." She scolded. "You should be ashamed of yourself, asking your poor widowed Mother for such an expensive thing, when you know she has to keep working in London amongst all the bombs and fires." I was suitably abashed.

Years later my Mother told me that owing to the lack of manpower during the war she was able to earn the highest wages she had ever had. In the event she had sent my present together with my sisters to Mr. Nuts address, so I had a nice surprise on Christmas morning.

Thursday morning, (market day) found us at the front door looking out for the farmer that Auntie dealt with to come into town, we soon spotted him and his wife trotting by in their pony and trap, and I followed on with Aunties large shopping basket down Belmont to their usual pitch in Broad St. There I paid for and collected her order of vegetables and a large pink goose. "Be sure to tell Miss Kedwards that I ave'nt drawn un," called the farmers wife as I left to hurry back to Ingle Nook with my precious load.

On Christmas eve my sisters came to tea and delivered my

present, not to be opened until the morning, later I helped Auntie to stuff and truss the goose ready to be cooked on Christmas morning by the baker at the top of Church Street, as our own oven was too small to take it. In the evening, with Mother tucked safely in bed and the two cats stretched out in front of the fire, having had their fill of boiled goose giblets, we played cards and ludo, listened to the wireless, made toast, and roasted chestnuts on the fire. Some may say that it wasn't exactly exciting, but I was happy enough.

Later in life I realised that I was probably her only company on those dark winter evenings and holiday times. Like most kids I was up early on Christmas day eager to open my presents, which turned out to be Rupert Bear and Beano annuals from Auntie, and a wonderful hand operated film projector from my Mother.

For Auntie Kit I had bought a wooden crucifix from the jewellers and gift shop down on the Pavement, paid for with money saved from my Saturday morning job. I was quite upset when on opening the box she started to cry, until she assured me that it was the best present she had ever been given. Then by the time we had laid and lit the fires, settled mother in the front room, and all had breakfast, it was time to deliver the goose. I watched as the baker slid it into the oven along with several others telling me at the same time that, when cooked he would bring it down to the house himself, as he thought it would be too hot for me to handle.

After dinner Auntie hung a sheet over the curtain rail in the back room to enable me to give a film show on my new toy. I set up the machine on the kitchen stool and some books to bring it level with the sheet, then with everything threaded up and in focus we brought Mother in to watch the show. The grainy sepia coloured film depicted four far eastern looking people dancing or stamping on straw or wheat. (I could never tell which) It only lasted two or three minutes so I rewound and played it through three times, sometimes in slow motion and then as fast as I could crank the handle, just to give my audience a laugh. After that, the sixty watt bulb inside the machine made the tin casing almost too hot to touch so we had to finish.

The rest of the afternoon was spent in the front room having tea and Christmas cake with Auntie playing softly on the piano ,while mother nodded gently by the fire. Boxing day was Sunday so we went to the chapel as usual where I dutifully pumped the organ for her to play. Then it was over.

A few months later I went home to a London that was still being bombarded by doodle bugs and V2 rockets. My days as an evacuee were over.

I realise now that throughout those years of austerity I can never remember being ill but as soon as the war was over I began to catch everything that was going. I caught chicken pox and scabies then pneumonia, after that it was a mild attack of polio that left me with a slightly withered right leg. During my national service in the far east, I managed to contract dengue fever and dhobi rash, since then I have suffered strains sprains torn ligaments broken bones, and dislocations, but of course, thanks to my Auntie Kit's good advice I have never suffered with chilblains.

The Return

In the late summer of 1946 I returned to Hay for a holiday with Auntie Kit, she greeted me like a long lost son, and in spite of my pleading refused to accept any payment for my keep, so I made up for that by having some good long stints in the garden, taking out all the weeds and generally tidying up. Auntie was getting on for sixty five years old at that time and still nursing her aged Mother and I realised that the garden was getting a bit much for her. She seemed so pleased to have my company again and eager for me tell her all about my life in London.

At the end of 1944 my family had moved from the small house in Bermondsey to a block of flats in Kennington, three bedrooms, inside toilet, proper bathroom, and the added luxury of electric lighting and power, (We had only gas lighting in Bermondsey.) so I could tell her how easy it was for me to watch cricket at the Oval, or take a ride on the tube to visit all the museums at Kensington and all the other sights, most of which were free entry. She was enthralled by it all, saying how she envied me as she had never been to London. I accompanied her to the shops once or twice and found it a bit embarrassing when she would remind all and sundry who I was. "What do you think of my little Teddy now then, hasn't he grown? And in long trousers too," she would say.

After a week in Hay and having visited all my old haunts I found things a bit tame and was ready for home, but there was something I wanted to do before I left. I was by now thirteen years old and over the last couple of years had become a good swimmer, so I was determined to swim across the Wye and back just for the challenge. I had intended to start my swim from the rapids on the Warren but found it too rough, so I set off from that little spit of flat rock that stretches out from the bank a few yards down stream.

I had never swam in a river before and was more than halfway across before I realised that the current had taken me a long way downstream. Fortunately a few more strokes took me into shallow water and a gap in the bank where cattle came down to drink. I thought that I could walk ashore but after a few steps found myself up to the knees in thick mud, so there was nothing for it but for me to keep close to the bank and wade upstream until I thought it safe enough to make the return crossing.

The swim back was much harder, as I now knew the strength of the current. I thought of old Gammy Dicks' warning and wanted to avoid being swept into the Steeple Pool, so it was hard going. I came ashore a little way down from my original starting point, exhausted but as proud as punch. Next day I went home.

It was to be quite a few years before I went back to Hay, what with joining the Boys Brigade, getting my first bike, starting my first job, and finding out about girls, the memories of my days as an evacuee faded away. Then came two years National Service spent mostly in the Far East servicing Sunderland flying boats, after that it was courting, marriage, and starting a family, the years slipped quickly by.

So it wasn't until 1962 when returning to London with my wife and one small son after a holiday in Tenby that I decided to turn off the A40 at Brecon and visit Auntie Kit. She greeted the little one in much the same manner as she had myself all those years ago with the offer of a nice piece of cake. We stayed awhile, had tea and explored the garden, then went on our way.

It was to be the last time I saw her. In 1970 I had occasion to pass through the town, and stopped to ask after her, only to be told that she was dead. I made further enquires with the local council and obtained the death certificate and found that she had died in the Mid Wales Hospital Talgarth on the 19th January 1970 aged 88, alone and perhaps by then a little dotty, and nobody that she knew there to see her off. I felt quite ashamed.

I did more research into Kate's early life, the results of which I have written into the foreword of this work, but it wasn't until the late nineties that I was persuaded by friends and family to put on record my time as an evacuee in world war two, even so it has taken a long time by anyone's standard for me to get everything together, and although the project has brought back many memories and given me great satisfaction I would really like it to be a dedication to that good woman, Kate Kedwards, my Auntie Kit.

Hay Changes

The immense changes that have taken place in the town since World War Two have made it a very different place to the one that I knew as an evacuee. The once sleepy market town has become a busy all year round tourist centre not only for outdoor pursuits like pony trekking canoeing, and hill walking, but also for its internationly famous literary festival which draws visitors from all over the world. This came into being after Mr. Booth made Hay the largest secondhand book centre in the world.

The continuous rise in the use of the motor car for personal travel was probably why the railway station and line to Hereford fell under Dr. Beechings' axe in 1963. Now the large car and coach park, together with the tourist information centre, toilets, gift shop and café off the Oxford Road make an excellent facility for the town.

The building of this complex is what probably caused the disappearance of the little stream that used to run down the side of Oxford Rd. It would disappear through a grill at the bottom of the street, surface again in front of the houses of Garibaldi Terrace, then dive under the road again to join the Dulas Brook from a culvert under the Cusop road bridge. I spent many a happy hour launching paper boats or twigs, then running across the road to see them come out the other end.

The path outside the town walls where the trolly met its demise runs from the behind the Black Lion pub and down to the bottom of Broad St. It was at one time five or six feet wide, but now disused and overgrown it can only be traversed by a single track through long grass alongside the fence. One of the more notable changes in the town is the presence of much more housing with several estates appearing on the outskirts, and on Belmont, where the Grant's garden used to be.

The cinema built post-war in what was once an empty field belonging to Mrs. Maddigan, and since made redundant through the rise and rise of television, is now probably the largest bookshop in the country. The old cinema used to be housed in a corrugated iron shed that was situated where what is now the industrial estate. And in place of the small lorry that was the fire engine garaged near the entrance to the mart, there is now the modern fire station built just past the cemetery.

Of course some things never change: the Norman tump still stands sentinel near St. Mary's church, unaltered, save for the posh wooden walkways that have been put in place for the benefit of tourist, and the spring at the Swan Well where once a small boy often slaked his thirst, still runs crystal clear, as it has done for hundreds of years. Long may it continue to do so.

The Author

At the Swan Well

On the steps of Inglenook